Bible Passages Bible Passages Bible Passages
Bible Passages Bible Passages Bible Passages
Bible Passages Bible Passages Bible Passages
Bible Passages Bible Passages Bible Passages
Bible Passages Bible Passages Bible Passages
Bible Passages Bible Passages Bible Passages
Bible Passages Bible Passages Bible Passages
Bible Passages Bible Passages Bible Passages
Bible Passages Bible Passages Bible Passages
Bible Passages Bible Passages Bible Passages
Bible Passages Bible Passages Bible Passages
Bible Passages Bible Passages Bible Passages
Bible Passages Bible Passages Bible Passages
Bible Passages Bible Passages Bible Passages
Bible Passages Bible Passages Bible Passages
Bible Passages Bible Passages Bible Passages
Bible Passages Bible Passages Bible Passages
Bible Passages Bible Passages Bible Passages
Bible Passages Bible Passages Bible Passages
Bible Passages Bible Passages Bible Passages
Bible Passages Bible Passages Bible Passages
Bible Passages Bible Passages Bible Passages
Bible Passages Bible Passages Bible Passages
Bible Passages Bible Passages Bible Passages
Bible Passages Bible Passages Bible Passages
Bible Passages Bible Passages Bible Passages
Bible Passages Bible Passages Bible Passages
Bible Passages Bible Passages Bible Passages
Bible Passages Bible Passages Bible Passages

This

book

belongs

to:

Allison Bittner

The New KIDS Book of

Bible Passages

The New Kids Book of Bible Passages

Copyright © 1999 Educational Publishing Concepts, Inc.,
Wheaton, IL

Published by New Kids Media™ in association with Baker
Book House Company, Grand Rapids, Michigan.

ISBN 0-8010-4434-0

Printed in the United States of America

1 2 3 4 — 02 01 00 99

The New KIDS Book of

Bible Passages

Anne Adams

Illustrated by Marlene McAuley

Published in
association with

For my children
Michal and Alexandra Tyra

Dear Parents,

It's never too early to begin teaching the truths of the Bible to your children. The Junior Reference Series will help young children understand the meaning of major Bible passages and see God's daily involvement in the lives of his people. They will enjoy learning about Bible animals and how their personalities were used to explain how people sometimes behave. Our prayer is that this series will instill in your child a lifelong thirst for knowledge of the Bible and it's message of love.

The Publishers

Isaiah 9:6

For to us a child is born, to us a son is given, and the government will be on his shoulders. And he will be called Wonderful Counselor, Mighty God, Everlasting Father, Prince of Peace.

God's love for us is so great, he sent his son Jesus to us. Jesus was once a child just like you. He grew up to be the light of the world. Where ever Jesus walked, darkness and evil fled. He is our Wonderful Counselor because he guides us, our Mighty God because he is more than able, our Everlasting Father because he will never leave us, and the Prince of Peace because he takes away our fears and fills us with calm!

JOHN 3:16

For God so loved the world that he gave his one and only Son, that whoever believes in him shall not perish but have eternal life.

God allowed his son Jesus to be crucified on the cross so you and I could be saved. When Jesus died on earth, he took all of our sins with him. He accepted our punishment, so we wouldn't have to suffer. If you truly believe in Jesus, you can have everlasting life. This means that when you die you will live again, just like Jesus did.

Your new home will be in heaven. Here, everything lives forever, even flowers! No one gets sick, there are no bad dreams, and everyone is happy!

Matthew 11:28-30

Come to me, all you who are weary and burdened, and I will give you rest. Take my yoke upon you and learn from me, for I am gentle and humble in heart, and you will find rest for your souls. For my yoke is easy and my burden is light.

A yoke is a piece of wood which fits over the shoulders of an ox. While the ox is wearing the yoke, he is able to pull heavy loads like a wagon or plow. Sometimes when we are troubled, we feel like the weight of the world is resting on our shoulders, just like a yoke. If you are sad, Jesus wants you to call out to him. He promises to take your burdens away and give you rest. His yoke is easy to wear. It is made of love and peace.

ROMANS 10:9

If you confess with your mouth, "Jesus is Lord," and believe in your heart that God raised him from the dead, you will be saved.

After Jesus died on the cross, his disciples thought he was gone forever. They didn't understand the meaning of eternal life. But Jesus rose from the dead just like he said he would. Then he went to heaven to be with his Father. Jesus made it easy for us to be saved and have this same eternal life. All we have to do is say, "Jesus is Lord," and believe that God raised him from the dead! Jesus died so we might have this salvation. What are we waiting for?

Matthew 19:14

Jesus said, "Let the little children come to me, and do not hinder them, for the kingdom of heaven belongs to such as these."

Jesus loves to be surrounded by children like you. Your faith and trust in him is so pure and simple. You don't need proof that he exists, you just know don't you?

Jesus didn't mean heaven is only for children. He meant that grownups need to have the same childlike faith in order to believe in him. Whoever humbles himself like a child is the greatest in the kingdom of heaven. Whoever welcomes a child, welcomes Jesus. But woe to those who cause a child to sin, because God says they will be punished.

1 John 1:8,9

If we claim to be without sin, we deceive ourselves and the truth is not in us. If we confess our sins, he is faithful and just and will forgive us our sins and purify us from all unrighteousness.

No one is perfect except Jesus. Have you ever made a mistake and sinned? Well, guess what? We all have. It is part of our human nature. God wants us to know that he understands. When we realize that we have sinned, all we have to do is confess our sins to God. He sees our hearts, he knows that we are sorry, and he always forgives us. God doesn't expect us to be perfect, he just wants us to try to do the right thing. He loves us, and he will never leave us. Even if we mess up sometimes.

PSaLM 119:105

Your word is a lamp to my feet and a light for my path.

Have you ever walked into a dark room and felt scared? If you carried a flashlight into the room, the beam of light would chase away the darkness. Sometimes life is just like a dark room. It can make us scared. God's Word, which is the Bible, is just like that flashlight. It lights up our path and chases away the darkness. Light and dark, like good and evil, cannot live together. When God's Word is in us, there is light. Darkness and evil have to go away. Thanks to Jesus, we never have to be afraid of the dark again!

Isaiah 55:11

*So is my word that goes out from my mouth:
It will not return to me empty, but will
accomplish what I desire and achieve the
purpose for which I sent it.*

God created the whole universe– the
planets, the sky, the stars and the oceans
–by speaking them into existence. His word
has the power to raise men from the dead
and heal the sick. God's Word is also filled
with promises for you and me. Since God is
perfect, he never breaks a promise. If God
says you have nothing to fear, you have
nothing to fear. His words are as true today
as they were years ago. They will remain
true forever. When you feel like the world
is changing around you, don't worry. God
and his Word will always stay the same.

Matthew 22:37-40

Love the Lord your God with all your heart and with all your soul and with all your mind. This is the first and greatest commandment. And the second is like it: Love your neighbor as yourself. All the Law and the Prophets hang on these two commandments.

There are many laws and rules, but Jesus said these two are the most important. If we truly love God with our whole being and love others like we love ourselves, we will naturally obey God's other commandments. Sometimes its hard to remember everything we are not supposed to do. God understands this. That's why he wants us to pay attention to what we are supposed to do. Its easy to remember–love God and love others.

1 JOHN 3:18

Dear children, let us not love with words or tongue but with actions and in truth.

The best way for us to let someone know that we love them is to show them rather than just tell them. What if someone told you that they loved you, but then they treated you badly. Would you feel loved? What if another person never said they loved you, but they did special things for you? Love is more than just words. God taught us the meaning of unconditional love when he sent his only son Jesus to die on the cross for us. He didn't just say he loved us, he proved it with his actions. Can you think of some special things you can do to show people that you truly love them?

1 Corinthians 13:4-8

Love is patient, love is kind. It does not envy, it does not boast, it is not proud. It is not rude, it is not self-seeking, it is not easily angered, it keeps no record of wrongs. Love does not delight in evil but rejoices with the truth. It always protects, always trusts, always hopes, always perseveres. Love never fails.

The kind of love that Jesus gives to you and me is called "unconditional love." This means that Jesus loves us perfectly no matter what we do or say. We don't have to do anything special in order for Jesus to love us. It's not easy to love others this way. It's something that we should strive for. Learn to be like Jesus, and someday you may be able to show this same kind of unconditional love to others.

GaLatiaNS 5:22, 23

*The fruit of the Spirit is love, joy, peace,
patience, kindness, goodness,
faithfulness, gentleness and self-control.
Against such things there is no law.*

When the Holy Spirit lives in us, he works
in us and makes us more like Jesus. Jesus is
loving, peaceful, patient, kind, good,
faithful, gentle and full of self-control.
These qualities are called fruit, and they can
grow in you, too. Get to know Jesus, love
him, remember him, and try to be like him.
God knows that is not always easy. It
pleases him when you ask for his help
Which of these fruit do you want the Spirit
to produce in you?

PSaLM 136:1

Give thanks to the LORD, for he is good. His love endures forever.

When we thank someone, we are showing them our appreciation for something they have done for us. Did you know that if you were the only person alive in the world, God would have sent Jesus to die on the cross just for you? That's how much he loves you. Jesus also forgives your sins, hears your prayers, comforts you when you are sad, guides you with his word, fills you with his spirit, and promises you everlasting life. He said his love will last forever. We have so much to be grateful for. Let's thank Jesus today for all he has done for us!

HebreWS 13:15

*Through Jesus, therefore, let us continually
offer to God a sacrifice of praise -
the fruit of lips that confess his name.*

One way we can thank God for all he has
done for us is to praise him. We can
praise him by singing songs to him, by
joyfully calling out his name, or simply by
doing something which shows how much
we love and appreciate him. Even the
angels in heaven circle the throne where
God sits and continually praise his name.
When you offer to God the sacrifice of
praise, especially when you don't feel like
it, your own spirit is lifted up and you feel
happy! God would love to hear your sweet
voice praising his name!

PHILIPPIANS 4:8

Whatever is true, whatever is noble, whatever is right, whatever is pure, whatever is lovely, whatever is admirable, if anything is excellent or praiseworthy - think about such things.

You know that if you eat healthy foods like apples and carrots, you will have a healthy body. The same is true of your mind. If you put healthy thoughts into your mind, you will have a healthy mind and a good attitude. You will be a joyful person, filled with peace and love. You probably won't even have bad dreams! So think of things which are true, noble, right, pure, lovely, admirable, excellent, and praiseworthy. Renew your mind with God's Word–it is filled with such lovely thoughts.

LuKe 6:37-38

Do not judge, and you will not be judged. Do not condemn, and you will not be condemned. Forgive, and you will be forgiven. Give, and it will be given to you. A good measure, pressed down, shaken together and running over, will be poured into your lap. For with the measure you use, it will be measured to you.

The way we treat others is the way we will be treated ourselves. God says that if you do something nice for someone, then someone will do something nice for you. If you forgive others, you'll be forgiven, too. If you show love, you'll be loved. We should treat others the same way that God treats us. He loves us. He is fair with us. He forgives us. He accepts us just the way we are.

JAMES 1:19-20

Everyone should be quick to listen, slow to speak and slow to become angry, for man's anger does not bring about the righteous life that God desires.

One of the hardest things in life to learn is how to be quiet and listen. It's hard for children, but it's also hard for grownups. All of us want to talk about our feelings. We want to shout when we are mad, we want to moan when we are sad, but we hardly ever want to just be quiet and listen. Only when you are very still can you hear God's voice. He speaks to us in the peaceful whisper of a breeze, not in the angry funnel of a tornado. Shhh. What do you hear?

MattheW 7:12

*So in everything, do to others
what you would have
them do to you.*

This is called the Golden Rule. The whole idea is to treat others exactly the way you want to be treated. Would you like it if someone made fun of you? I bet it would make you sad. Well, that means that you should never make fun of anyone else.

Would you like it if you were feeling bad and someone took the time to comfort you? That means you should try to be a friend to someone when they need extra love. What are some other things that you enjoy that you can do for other people?

JaMeS 4:7

Submit yourselves, then, to God. Resist the devil, and he will flee from you.

God is the greatest power and authority in the whole world. Nothing is above him, especially not the devil. His power can't begin to compare to God's power. Since God lives in you, you have power over the devil. You can tell bad dreams to go away. You can tell scary thoughts to leave you alone. You can tell the devil to scram—and he will! Remember that the God which lives in you is bigger than anything in the world. Stay close to God where you'll be safe and tell the devil to go away. There is nothing to fear when you stay close to God.

PHiLiPPiaNS 4:6-7

Do not be anxious about anything, but in everything, by prayer and petition, with thanksgiving, present your requests to God. And the peace of God which transcends all understanding, will guard your hearts and your minds in Christ Jesus.

Did you know that you have a best friend? This best friend never gets mad at you. He never makes you feel bad about yourself. He loves the sound of your voice. He cares about how you feel, and he longs to spend time with you. His name is Jesus. When you are sad or worried about anything at all, Jesus wants you to pray. When you talk to him, God takes your fears away from you. Then the sweet peace of Jesus fills you up!

Matthew 7:7-8

Ask and it will be given to you; seek and you will find; knock and the door will be opened to you. For everyone who asks receives; he who seeks finds; and to him who knocks, the door will be opened.

God's arms are always open. They are always ready to welcome us, to love us, to comfort us, and to guide us. If you ask anything of God, you will surely receive it. If you search for God, you will always find him. If you knock on his door, he will always be home, and the door will always be open to you. You don't need a special key to find God. You don't need a map or even a compass. Your heart will guide you to him. Go quickly! He is waiting for you!

JaMeS 1:5-6

If any of you lacks wisdom, he should ask God, who gives generously to all without finding fault, and it will be given to him. But when he asks, he must believe and not doubt, because he who doubts is like a wave of the sea, blown and tossed by the wind.

Wisdom is all about having good sense and judgment. You can be very smart, but still lack wisdom. Its about knowing what to do with the knowledge you have. Smarts, good looks, and money are all meaningless without wisdom. God will give you wisdom if you ask for it, just like he gave it to King Solomon. But when you ask for anything from God, you have to believe that you will receive it. God wants you to put your faith in him. Trust him. He never breaks a promise. His word is always true.

PSALM 27:1

*The Lord is my light and my salvation–
whom shall I fear? The Lord is the
stronghold of my life– of whom shall I be
afraid?*

Fear is like a dark shadow. It creeps along
the walls of our mind. Everyone has been
afraid of things at certain times. Some
people are afraid of the dark while some are
afraid of spiders. Others are afraid of
thunderstorms. Are you afraid of
something?

Jesus has great news for you. He is
bigger and stronger than any fear you may
have. He is your protector. He will keep
you safe. Jesus is the light which chases
away the dark shadows of fear. If God is on
your side, what do you have to be afraid of?

NeHeMiaH 8:10

Do not grieve, for the joy of the LORD is your strength.

Lots of times, we will feel sad, frustrated, and hurt. The world we live in right now is not like heaven. People are not perfect, and nothing here lasts forever. But because you know Jesus, you have a reason to rejoice! Even when your friends or family let you down, you can be assured that God will neve leave you. When you are afraid, you know a God who is more than able. When you are sad, you know a God who comforts.

Pain, fear, and sadness won't last, but God will! He's with you through it all, forever and ever. This is a reason to be joyful. This joy will keep you strong and lift you out of your sadness.

HebreWS 2:18

Because he himself suffered when he was tempted, he is able to help those who are being tempted.

Jesus is the son of God, but while he was on earth he lived as a man. His body was flesh and blood just like yours. He had feelings just like you do. He felt happy and excited. He felt loving and tender. He also felt mad, sad, hurt, worried, and afraid.

Jesus understands everything you are feeling, because he felt it, too. He knows what it means to be tempted, because he was tempted in every way. When you need help doing the right thing, talk to your friend Jesus. He knows just what you are going through and he will help you.

1 Corinthians 10:13

No temptation has seized you except what is common to man. And God is faithful; he will not let you be tempted beyond what you can bear. But when you are tempted, he will also provide a way out so that you can stand up under it.

There is not one person on earth who has not been tempted to do wrong. You will be faced with temptations your whole life, even when you grow up. You might be tempted to disobey your parents, or to lie, or to take something which is not yours. God wants you to know that with his help, it is possible to "say no" to those temptations. Run away from anything you know is wrong. Choose to do what is right. The most important thing of all is to pray to God. He will set your feet on the right path and keep you strong along the way.

PSaLM 18:16-17

He reached down from on high and took hold of me; he drew me out of deep waters. He rescued me from my powerful enemy, from my foes, who were too strong for me.

It's easy to feel like we are drowning in deep water when we are troubled. We feel helpless and weak. We don't know what to do. But there is always something you can do. You can call out to Jesus, your heavenly father. When you do, he rushes to help you. He pulls you out of those deep waters. He gently lifts you to solid ground then steps between you and your enemies so they cannot hurt you. He surrounds you with his love and protection. He hides you in his arms.

Matthew 5:43-44

You have heard that it was said, "Love your neighbor and hate your enemy.'" But I tell you: Love your enemies and pray for those who persecute you.

Some people are not very nice. They may call us names, tease us, or tell lies about us. Their actions are wrong. It's never all right to mistreat someone else. When someone treats you badly, its natural to want to hurt them back. Its okay to feel mad and hurt, but you shouldn't treat them the same way they treated you. Pray that God will help them. Let the love of Jesus replace your anger. God doesn't expect you to feel loving, but with his help you may be able to show them the love of Jesus. Then you will be like a shining light in a world of darkness.

Matthew 10:29-31

Are not two sparrows sold for a penny? Yet not one of them will fall to the ground apart from the will of your Father. And even the very hairs of your head are all numbered. So don't be afraid; you are worth more than many sparrows.

God sees everything. He is aware of what happens to each and every sparrow. He knows when the robins lay their eggs in the spring, when a drop of water splashes to the pavement, when a leaf floats to the grass. If he sees all of these things, do you think he doesn't know what happens to you each and every day? He watches with delight as you run and jump and play. He feels your displeasure when you've had a bad day. He is ready and able to help you when you are afraid. Don't be. He is there!

Matthew 6:19-21

Do not store up for yourselves treasures on earth, where moth and rust destroy, and where thieves break in and steal. But store up for yourselves treasures in heaven, where moth and rust do not destroy, and where thieves do not break in and steal. For where your treasure is, there your heart will be also.

Money is nice to have because it buys things that we need. It gives us food, and clothes, and even a place to live. It's also fun to have nice things, like toys. But what if a robber came in and took many of your things? What would you be left with? You would be left with the most important thing of all. Jesus. Your salvation is the greatest treasure you will ever have, and it can't be bought with money.

Matthew 5:14-16

You are the light of the world. A city on a hill cannot be hidden. Neither do people light a lamp and put it under a bowl. Instead, they put it on its stand, and it gives light to everyone in the house. In the same way, let your light shine before men, that they may see your good deeds and praise your Father in heaven.

Have you ever seen a lighthouse? Its powerful light helps guide ships safely to shore in dark or foggy weather. Jesus wants you to be like a lighthouse. He wants his light to shine from you so brightly that those who are lost will be drawn to you. They will see the light of Jesus in you and find their way. If you act like Jesus and talk about him, your light will always burn bright.

Matthew 7:15-17

Watch out for false prophets. They come to you in sheep's clothing, but inwardly they are ferocious wolves. By their fruit you will recognize them . . . every good tree bears good fruit, but a bad tree bears bad fruit.

Just because people talk about Jesus, doesn't mean they actually know and love him. Not everyone is true and honest and good. Jesus is our shepherd and we are his sheep, but sometimes a wolf dressed up like a sheep sneaks into the fold. If you want to know who the true sheep are, look at them more closely. True sheep don't just dress like sheep, they act like sheep. They don't just talk like sheep, they live like sheep.

Matthew 19:30

But many who are first will be last, and many who are last will be first.

In our world, people who are very rich, very famous, or very powerful are often loved or admired the most. Those who simply love Jesus are sometimes made fun of. Christians serve Jesus not because they will receive praise from the world, but because they will be honored in heaven. Its all right to be rich and famous as long as we honor Jesus with our lives. Those who don't will have to be happy with their worldly treasures, because they won't receive any in heaven. Will you store up your treasures in heaven or on earth?

Ecclesiastes 11:1

Cast your bread upon the waters, for after many days you will find it again.

Have you ever been to the seashore? The tide washes up many unusual treasures: sea shells, bottles, chunks of glass worn smooth by the waves, drift wood.

Each time you do something good and work hard, you are casting your bread upon the water. God says you will find it again and when you do, it will be like a treasure that comes out of the sea. Your work will be smooth and refined like a piece of glass. If you seize every chance you can to do your best, good things and unexpected pleasures will be returned to you. Nothing good comes easy and nothing is free. Even your salvation came at a price.

Proverbs 3:5-6

Trust in the LORD with all your heart and lean not on your own understanding; in all your ways acknowledge him, and he will make your paths straight.

People get so busy with their own lives, they forget all about God. They get used to doing things a certain way, they feel pretty good, and–wham–something happens! Then they remember to pray and ask God for guidance!

Wouldn't it be easier if we didn't wait so long to look to God for direction? God wants you to seek him daily. Trust him daily. Live your life for him daily. If you do this, he will guide your footsteps, and you will never stray down the wrong path.

PSaLM 37:4

Delight yourself in the LORD and he will give you the desires of your heart.

To know Jesus is to love him. He is gentle, patient, sweet, and compassionate. He is mercy and grace. He is tender, he is love, he is peace. He is the Alpha and the Omega—the beginning and the end. When we know him, we can't help but delight ourselves in him. When we delight ourselves in him, we can't help but commit our lives to him. When we commit our lives to him, he can't help but give us the desires of our heart!

PHiLiPPiaNS 4:12-13

I know what it is to be in need, and I know what it is to have plenty. I have learned the secret of being content in any and every situation, whether well fed or hungry, whether living in plenty or in want. I can do everything through him who gives me strength.

Nothing is perfect all of the time. Sometimes you probably wish you had more of something good. Or you might wish you had less of something not so good. Perhaps you're feeling bad about something that happened today. Everyone has these feelings.

The important thing to remember is that life is never perfect. Try to do the right thing each day and when life is hard, ask God to make you extra strong. He will.

Deuteronomy 28:3-6

You will be blessed in the city and blessed in the country. The fruit of your womb will be blessed, and the crops of your land and the young of your livestock . . . . Your basket and your kneading trough will be blessed. You will be blessed when you come in and blessed when you go out.

Some people think that when you serve the Lord, you have to give up everything good in life. That is not so. If you serve the Lord and obey his commands, God promises to bless you. He will give you happiness and good fortune wherever you go. He even promises to bless your children! Everything which you put your hands to will be blessed, and you will never be without.

Isaiah 40:31

Those who hope in the Lord will renew their strength. They will soar on wings like eagles; they will run and not grow weary, they will walk and not be faint.

Even the strongest people get tired at times, but we serve a God who never loses his strength or power. God is never too tired, too busy, too sick, or too impatient to listen to you. He is there whenever you need him, even in the middle of the night! Because God is so strong and tireless, he is able to give us some of his strength when we are weak. He helps us run the race of life without getting too tired out!

PSaLM 23:1-4

The LORD is my shepherd, I shall not be in want. He makes me lie down in green pastures, he leads me beside quiet waters, he restores my soul. He guides me in paths of righteousness for his name's sake. Even though I walk through the valley of the shadow of death, I will fear no evil, for you are with me; your rod and your staff, they comfort me.

Jesus is the good shepherd and we are his sheep. He cares for us so we want for nothing. He puts our feet on the right path and leads us gently to the right places. If one sheep wanders away and gets lost, be assured—Jesus will find him. He cares for even the smallest sheep, like you. He will quench your thirst, restore your soul, protect you, and comfort you. Follow him always. He is the only true shepherd.

Other books in this series include:

The New Kids Book of Bible People

The New Kids Book of Bible Animals

The New Kids Book of Angel Visits